Brain Training:

How to Improve Focus, Concentration, Memory, IQ and Start to Think Faster

By

Eva Delano

Table of Contents

Introduction 5

Chapter 1. Let's Start from The Beginning 6

Chapter 2. How to Train Our Brain 8

Chapter 3. Signs of Brain Deteriorating 11

Chapter 4. How to Improve Your Memory 13

Chapter 5. How to Think Faster 15

Chapter 6. How to Increase Your Attention Span 17

Chapter 7. Brain Training Tips 18

Chapter 8. How To Boost Your IQ (Intelligence Quotient) 23

Chapter 9. Brain Training Facts 27

Chapter 10. Brain Training and Degenerative Diseases 28

Chapter 11. Both Sides Of The Story 29

Conclusion 30

Thank You Page 31

Brain Training: How to Improve Focus, Concentration, Memory, IQ and Start to Think Faster

By Eva Delano

© Copyright 2014 Eva Delano

Reproduction or translation of any part of this work beyond that permitted by section 107 or 108 of the 1976 United States Copyright Act without permission of the copyright owner is unlawful. Requests for permission or further information should be addressed to the author.

This publication is designed to provide accurate and authoritative information in regard to the subject matter covered. This work is sold with the understanding that the publisher is not engaged in rendering legal, accounting, or other professional services. If legal advice or other expert assistance is required, the services of a competent professional person should be sought.

First Published, 2014

Printed in the United States of America

Introduction

For the last few years the term "brain training" seems to appear everywhere: in the news, at schools etc. Everybody is talking about it, but what is brain training? Can we really train the brain? This book will help you to find the answers.

As we know aging doesn't stop and like every other part of our body brain suffers it too, suddenly we start forgetting about things like phone numbers or people's names. Some other times we can't find our keys or cell phones and we can think it's because of our busy lives but the truth is that our brain is getting old. Memory issues are related with degeneration and lost of cognitive skills. It sounds awful, but don't worry there are many activities we can do to train our brain and help it to improve its function, here we will analyze them and will mention some ideas about how to get a better concentration, improve our memory, think faster and avoid distractions.

Chapter 1. Let's Start from The Beginning

When a baby is born, the brain has one hundred billion neurons linked among each other, two years later at age three the neurons have been duplicated in number. Have you ever heard the phrase "kids are like sponges"? That is because children learn from everything near them, in their environment they find a big opportunity for brain training, just the fact of touching cold or hot water, tasting a new food, listening to the sound of a bell, all these experiences are training the child's brain. Many years ago children were no stimulated in the same way they are now. New mothers are stimulating babies even before they born, since fetus they are listening classical music, they listen to their parents reading stories. It is known now that if parents speak to their children when they are still in the uterus, the children will learn approximately three hundred more words at the age of two. Newborns are able to distinguish "words" from other sounds like a bell ring for example. All of these as a result of constant stimulation parents are giving them.

Nowadays-early stimulation is extremely important for how a child will learn in the future; it could change the whole way in which a student will develop at school. In present times there are gyms for toddlers that help them developing physical and cognitive skills, they learn through music, sensory activities, cause and effect experiences.

As we get old we lose the ability to connect our neurons, because of the activities we realized, they are more mechanical, our brain is used to do them, like brushing our teeth, or driving a car, but what if we introduce some new activities, some activities that challenge our brain to think again, not just to respond automatically? If we don't use our brain we are going to lose it.

Chapter 2. How to Train Our Brain

Brain training is not like a magic formula that scientists have discovered during the last years that will make you smarter instantly, what brain training is about is to make you better or more capable to perform tasks, to improve memory and attention span as well as fast thinking.

What is memory? It is the brain's ability to store information and it can do it in different ways: by recognition, verbal or episodic.

What is attention? It's the brain's ability to focus while avoiding unwanted distractions.

What is fast thinking? It's the ability to react to certain circumstances and provide solutions.

Each activity we do to challenge our brain will stimulate it and will contribute to build capacity. Brain is constantly adapting to different situations through life but those who challenge it are helping us to prevent brain degeneration, a person who is highly active will boost its brain while a person who receives less stimulation has a higher percentage to develop a degenerative disease like Alzheimer. Then less talk and more practice.

First of all training the brain is like training your muscles, if you want to improve your core for example, well, you must do some crunches, not all exercises have the same purpose and goals. The same happens with the brain it will depend on which brain function you think needs more improvement. A target needs to be set, concentration, cognitive skills, or social activities just to mention a few. These exercises will provide benefits such as memory, attention, brain speed, and intelligence. The better our brain register information, the respond to it will be greater, this way we could store information and use it later, it is important to focus on small details and use all five senses. If a brain is not aware of details in our common life, it will slow down. During our whole life our brain absorb lots of information through senses; sounds, feelings, shapes but at the age of thirty our brain starts to "switch off" and there is where problems begin: it think less, missed details, is not so fast anymore and processing information is turned into a slow process, understanding is more difficult too. When these signs first appeared we are not so aware of them, but as time goes by gaps are bigger and more difficult to fill them, there is when we start wondering what is going on with us. The first explanation we give ourselves is because we are too busy with our lives, or maybe to tired, maybe we just weren't paying attention, but the truth is our brain begins to get older. What to do then? Can we prevent it? Can we delay it?

Chapter 3. Signs of Brain Deteriorating

Here is a list of things we should be aware of; maybe some signs of a future develop of a degenerative disease:

1) Having memory lapses commonly

2) Having difficulty in performing tasks we are used to do on a daily basis

3) Forgetting names, phone numbers, and having trouble putting sentences together (last one will be a more damage condition)

4) Lost objects or being disoriented.

5) Having poor judgment, struggling with cause and effect situations.

6) Difficulties at completing activities that require abstract thinking.

7) Leave things in places where they don't belong. For example placing the toothpaste in the fridge.

8) Having mood changes without a reason.

9) Changes in people's personality. This one shows a more damage condition too.

10) Become passive.

Chapter 4. How to Improve Your Memory

Every bit of information in our memory is connected, our memory works by association, we associate experiences, objects and people, for example if you think about the word fish you immediately associate it with water, or the word watch you think about what time is it. If there were no association between the information we receive, it would be very difficult for us to remember things.

So why do people have bad memory? The answer is easy, we have a good memory but we don't use it efficiently, the key to have a good memory is to practice using it. Then what can you do to learn to remember things in a better way? The answer is creating association! If there is something you need to remember associate it with something else you believe will help you remembering. For example if you need to buy something for dinner associate it with the supermarket or think about yourself eating that specific food. This way it will be easy for you to remember before the information fades from the short-term memory. Sometimes it won't be so fast because there is information that is not so easy to associate; here comes the challenge to the brain, the idea is to be creative and make that brain think beyond, of course you are not going to create a whole story every time you want to remember something, just some pictures here and there. Practicing these kind of exercises will launch your brain into a new level; now that we know how memory works let's take advantage of that property.

Chapter 5. How to Think Faster

Have you ever been in a situation in which you need to give a fast answer but your brain seems to be blank? You try to look there for the correct answer but you can't find it so fast. For some people, commonly adults result difficult to think fast, it takes a while for the brain to search the information and processes it. Again, it is all about brain training, the same as a person trains to run faster in a race, the same way it can train to think faster. Here is the how to:

1) Relax It is the first thing you need to do. If you have hundreds of thoughts in your mind at the same, it will be cluttered and you will be frustrated trying to filter the information. Just breath, calm down and think about that specific information you are looking for. Try this exercise frequently; while working just stop for a minute and solve a three digit addition or a multiplication as fast as you can, then go back to your work. Two weeks later you will see a big improvement in your response time.

2) Analyze The objective is to think faster and answer faster yes, but also the purpose is that the brain looks for the correct information. Some reasoning games will help with this. Look for games where you have three or more possible solutions to a problem, choose the one that best suits in a short period of time, beat that clock!

3) Be creative Creativity is a great brain booster. Maybe you are not such a creative person but try writing down a story, each day you can write down a page within a month you will have a complete story. Children are very creative; this contributes to their fast learning of things, give a boost to your imagination and let it go. Who knows you can turn into a famous novelist.

4) Use the map You are trying to understand that history topic you need for school and it seems going nowhere in your mind. A good resource will be to use a mind mapping where you can visualize the information and store it. Later when you need to think fast about that homework your brain will recall the image for you faster.

Chapter 6. How to Increase Your Attention Span

Are you that kind of person that distracts with a fly passing by? Is your attention span very short? Can't you get focus? It is known that people who can work for hours without distracting get better jobs but don't worry there's still a solution.

1) Good morning If it is difficult for you to focus try to do whatever is most important early in the mornings, when you are sharper and with more energy. While day goes by we are getting engage with too many activities and it will be difficult to focus in what is really important.

2) Exclusivity If you have a very important task to develop, dedicate some quality time to it and ignore other external factors. You will finish sooner without stressing.

Stress causes loss of attention.

3) Schedule Find the way to schedule your activities, it is not the same being worried to finish one thing than twenty! Assign a determine time according to each activity this way you will be able to cope with all of them. When you are doing something remember to just focus in that activity. Believe me, your brain will thank you.

Chapter 7. Brain Training Tips

The brain is not designed to be multitask although people want to do everything at the same time. Imagine a woman who is carrying a baby on her arm while she is talking on the cell phone, doing laundry, cooking...poor brain. Yes she did all that stuff but then she couldn't remember where she put the keys, she forgot to feed the dog and she couldn't concentrate later when she tried to finish her work. Did you catch the idea?

There are some very easy activities or tasks to get started, things you have never imaging that will help you to make you brain fit and are available at your everyday life. Go on and take notes about these important facts.

1) Change your diet. There are some foods you can eat to improve brain function. We can't not mention all of them but these are very important to consider them, **berries** protect brain from oxidation, this reduces age related conditions like dementia or Alzheimer, **wild salmon** is full of omega 3 which is great for brain function, **nuts and seeds** contain great amounts of Vitamin E that help to lessen cognitive decline, **dark chocolate** helps the brain to release dopamine which allows memory storage and learning functions, **bananas** have a significant amount of vitamin that reduces risk of Parkinson's disease.

2) Go on a field trip. Try to visit a place of your interest at least once a week. Pay careful attention to details. Next day reconstruct the trip maybe by writing an essay including all details you remember. Activities like thinking and remembering will improve brain functions. Enjoy the experience!

3) Memorize. A good training for the brain will be memorizing a song or a poem, repeat it until you memorize and then write it down. Having better listening habits will active memory and help focus.

4) Play an instrument. Again listening skills are used to improve movements control according to sound as well as memorizing.

5) Put those hands and eyes to work. Try some hand-eye coordination activities for example throw a ball and catch it. Your brain will respond to this action. These kind of activities will improve fast thinking and the way we response to a determine situation.

6) Exercise your vision. Just sit in a place which can be indoors or outdoors, stare straight and concentrate, focus in every object, person, you can see, a minute later write down a list about all things you can remember. Stare again and check with your list. This will help a neurotransmitter called acetylcholine to develop attentiveness.

7) Change your hand. Use your other hand, do some activities that represent a challenge for example writing or eating. Learning new movements will help neurons to connect. When you become good at the activity, change it.

8) Move that body. Exercise! There are many benefits for the brain because of exercise, the hippocampus get stimulated and improves memory and learning ability. A healthy brain creates new cells. Exercise also makes heart pumps more oxygen to the brain improving brain cells growth. It also stimulates brain's plasticity creating new connections between neurons.

9) Catch a good sleep. Getting a good sleep will bring lots of benefits, while sleeping brain consolidates memories and sends information to the "long term memory section". If you don't sleep well probably you will have learning problems. This is why is very important for children to rest well so they can focus at school.

10) Read. Reading is a great activity for brain training; try reading genres you are not used to; like a science article or poetry. Read out loud and be aware of what you are reading, analyze the information.

11) Get social. In the same way exercise is important, having social interaction is very important for cognitive sharpness. Try to established long period relationships, join a fitness club, have a reunion with your college classmates, established a weeknight to do an activity with friends, be happy!

12) Learn a foreign language. If you really want to challenge your brain try to learn a new language, this would implied to think, write and speak in a different way you are used to. Being bilingual will duplicate the challenge to the brain. Now imagine if you learn three languages!

13) Meditate. When people think about brain training they associated it with exercise, moving, being active and I know you are thinking right now how could meditate will help brain training while being in a relaxed and calmed state, well meditation improves the ability of the brain to deal with stress. If you are not stressed your brain won't be stress and you will be able to focus better.

14) Take a walk Humans are always thinking, even if we don't notice it, all those mental conversations could interfere with constructive thoughts. Go for walk, get some fresh air, refresh your mind. Maybe at first you will be thinking about lots of things but as you continue you will be able to clear your mind.

15) Laugh! Did you know that laughter improves your brain function? Laughing is a great brain training exercise; it stimulates both sides of the brain at the same time, (few actions do this) so what about laughing more often.

As you see this activities aren't difficult and don't take a lot of time, they can be practiced by children or elder people. You can easily start practicing them before to move on with a more challenging ones.

We have talked about changing habits to improve memory, learning abilities, how to focus in a better way; now let's take it to the next level.

Chapter 8. How To Boost Your IQ (Intelligence Quotient)

IQ is measured by a series of standardized tests to compare intelligence among humans. IQ is part genetics and part environmental but is true that it can be rise. How can we accomplish it? Here comes the fun part, you can increase your IQ by playing games and there is a wide variety of them. Again these activities applied for children or grown ups.

1) Sudoku. Many people referred to Sudoku as a game, some others describe it like a mental activity. Sudoku helps improving speed, it involves visual perception, logic, concentration, and hand-eye coordination. It's a great activity for children, they can practice math at the same time they are boosting their IQ. Also is a recommended activity for elders to prevent memory loss.

2) Logic Games. It is important to have good logical skills. These abilities involved solving mathematics problems, understand cause and effect in the environment that surround us, and how to make deductions in a rational way. Examples of logical games are chess, mazes, problem solving, all of these are great for kids and they can be used as an everyday activity in the classroom. Tetris is an example of a great logic game.

3) Video Games. We live in the video games era and it is not exclusive for children, grown ups can enjoy them at the same time they are boosting their brain. Maybe it will not be easier to play a video game for a mom as it is for her child, but she could improve all the way to become an expert. Video games are great stimulation for the brain that makes it improve strategic thinking. It will be good to switch games every now and then and to avoid playing always the same one, or the ones you already know.

4) Cryptology. It is the activity of figure out codes (using letters, numbers or both) and solving them. This is good for logic and lateral thinking.

5) Solve Puzzles. It could be a classic jigsaw puzzle, a riddle, or a crossword puzzle even a word search it doesn't matter which one do you prefer. Crossword and word search puzzles are excellent to solve in a free time, for example while waiting for somebody, or as an activity in the classroom depending on kids age range there are different kinds of puzzles.

6) Trivia Games. Everybody once in live has watched a television show where contestants have to answer correctly to win, and while watching the show from home everybody is giving the correct. Well the task here is to play not just to watch, you can do it online or with a group of friends or family.

7) Strategic Games. These kinds of games involved a lot of thinking where people have to analyze certain situations; such a good exercise for the brain. Some strategic games are chess, checkers risk.

8) Play Cards. Keep your mind sharp by playing cards. Play bridge and encourage thought about strategy, play poker and boost the ability to determine probabilities even if you are alone you can play solitary.

It is important for you to know that when you become expert at a particular skill your brain training will stop, you will have reached a certain objective, so when this happens choose another challenging activity and boost your brain again. Keep learning. Activities should be challenging, this way they will provoke chemical changes in the brain; these chemicals contribute to learning and memorize. Activities should be progressive, again, from an easy level to become a master working through the entire process.

Are you thinking you are running out of activities? There is always something new at the horizon: Learn a new language, take ballroom classes, learn how to knit, engage your brain systems!

Chapter 9. Brain Training Facts

The are some interesting facts about brain training that you would be interested in reading them:

a) Active and well-stimulated neurons get more oxygen and assimilate in a better way more nutrients.

b) Receiving and adequate stimulation multiplies connections between synapses (connections between nerves cells)

c) Want to generate new neurons? The key is being mentally active; it will generate some new neurons, develop them and help them to survive through aging.

d) Age doesn't matter; neurons are able to regenerate using stem cells.

e) Brain training can help with learning problems such ADHD, dyslexia or autism.

f) Average people only uses 10% of their brain's capacity. Why don't improve it?

g) Babies lose half of their neurons before they are born even when they have 100 billion neurons at birth.

h) If you want to strengthen synapses avoid alcohol, stress and other toxins.

Chapter 10. Brain Training and Degenerative Diseases

Brain Training is more effective when it is offered in an early stage of life, when symptoms are absent or mild, but it could help in a certain way.

Can brain training prevent Alzheimer and dementia? Studies have shown benefits from an active brain. Games, puzzles and other brain training activities help slow mental decline. We are talking here about prevention, It is not proven that a patient with Alzheimer or dementia get better while already having such condition, loss memory is irreparable that is the reason why prevention is such important.

Chapter 11. Both Sides Of The Story

As adults were are constantly searching for a youth fountain and we will do it whatever its in our reach to keep us young both body and mind. Brain training represents a hope against brain degeneration. As parents or teachers brain training is a great solution to help children in their learning struggling. As an industry brain training represents millions of dollars each year. Of course there's a controversy about brain training, while it become a multimillionaire industry, some experts affirm spending money and time playing "those games" is not going to help improving brain's ability, it will also improve the ability to play an specific game.

On the other hand the owners of certain companies claim each one of their games are based on science and many years of research and population tests.

In my humble opinion brain training does exist, and as I mention before brain is like any other muscle in our body, it needs to be exercise, fed and nurture.

Conclusion

Many years ago a fifty year old person was considered and old person, living in retirement with no more exciting future, well that was past and in present days people in their 60's, 70's can have a brain of a thirty year old. They are getting more interested in other activities, they exercise, study, travel, and the result of this stimulation: a healthier brain.

Prevention is in your hands, don't let aging defeat you, many resources are out there waiting to being used, there is no need to spend big amounts of money. Brain training is an excellent opportunity to have a long and high quality life. It is our responsibility to help children and young people to improve their learning, to have a life full of stimulus that delay aging and degenerative diseases.

The option is yours, to believe or not believe in brain training benefits, at least give it a try, just by changing your daily habits you are boosting your brain.

Thank You Page

I want to personally thank you for reading my book. I hope you found information in this book useful and I would be very grateful if you could leave your honest review about this book. I certainly want to thank you in advance for doing this.

www.ingramcontent.com/pod-product-compliance
Lightning Source LLC
LaVergne TN
LVHW021946060526
838200LV00042B/1933